For Henry.
—HB

To Paul and Lucile,
my two little pumpkins.
—CA

Published by Sourcebooks eXplore, an imprint of Sourcebooks Kids
P.O. Box 4410, Naperville, Illinois 60567-4410
(630) 961-3900
sourcebookskids.com
Cataloging-in-Publication Data is on file with the Library of Congress.
Source of Production: Toppan Leefung Printing Co., Ltd., Dongguan, Guangdong Province, China
Date of Production: January 2024
Run Number: 5037235
Printed and bound in China.
TL 10 9 8 7 6 5 4 3 2 1

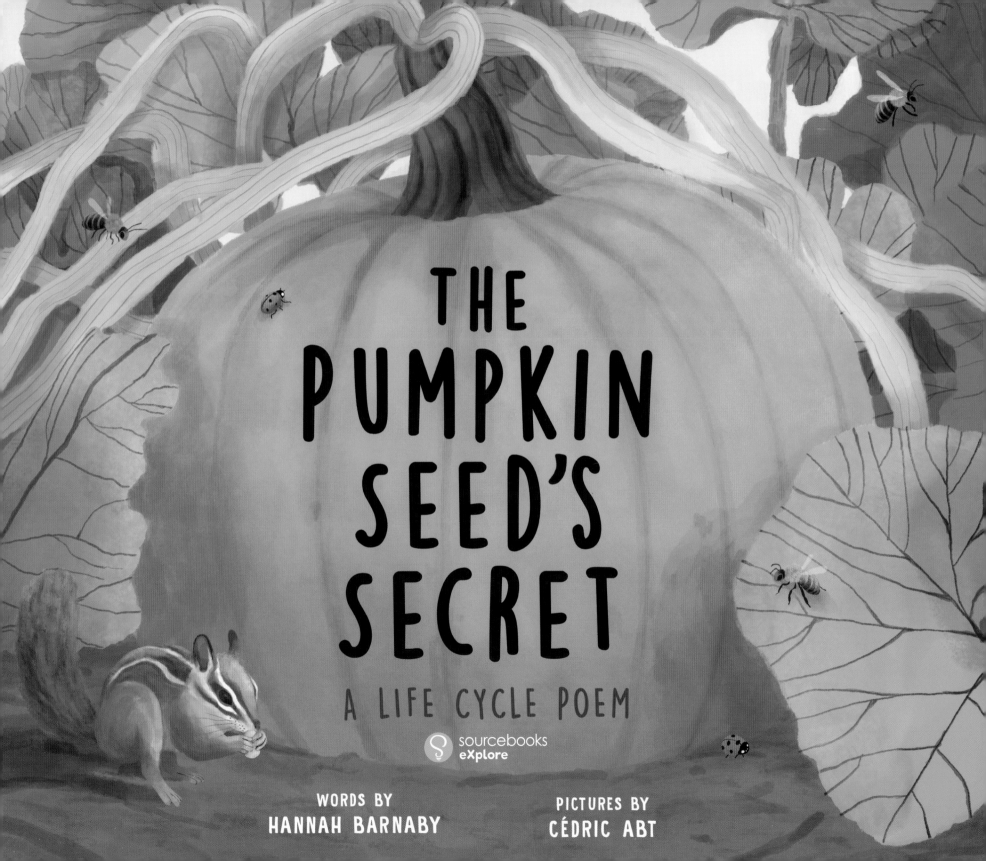

THE PUMPKIN SEED'S SECRET

A LIFE CYCLE POEM

sourcebooks
eXplore

WORDS BY
HANNAH BARNABY

PICTURES BY
CÉDRIC ABT

A pumpkin is a seed.
A plain little seed with a secret inside,
A pocket, a pip with a new life to hide.

To hide and to hold
As springtime unfolds,
A pumpkin begins as a seed.

A pumpkin is a sprout.
A curious sprout with one leaf and then two,
A budding, a nudging, a slow peekaboo.

Happy for rain
And sunshine again,
A pumpkin pops out as a sprout.

A pumpkin is a vine.
A traveling vine crawling over the ground,
Leafy and reaching and stretching around,

A deeply green loom
Where the blossoms will bloom,
A pumpkin grows into a vine.

A pumpkin is a flower.
Velvety petals with ruffles and seams,
Orangey-yellow as summer sunbeams.

The garden's best gown,
Calling honeybees down,
A pumpkin turns into a flower.

A pumpkin is a fruit.
A round little fruit growing larger each day,
A globe, a whole world in its own quiet way.

Painting orange on green,
Setting autumn, a scene,
A pumpkin swells into a fruit.

A pumpkin is a face.
Plucked just in time for a spooky display,
A smile that beguiles or scares us away.

A signal, a light,
On a Halloween night,
A pumpkin turns into a face.

A pumpkin is a food.
Bake it or cake it or cut it to roast.
Pie it, puree it, or spread it on toast.

You might be suspicious,
But oh, it's delicious!
A pumpkin makes excellent food.

A pumpkin is a house.
Leave it outdoors, and watch to see who:
Some slugs and some bugs, or a chipmunk or two.

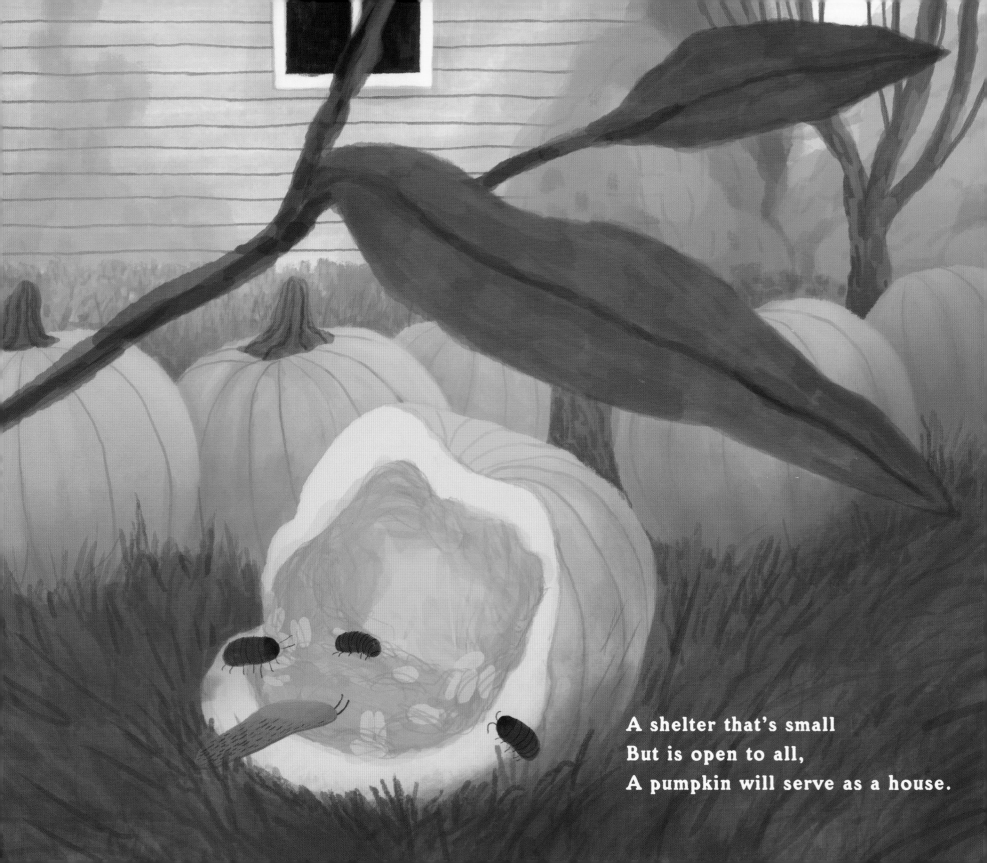

A shelter that's small
But is open to all,
A pumpkin will serve as a house.

A pumpkin is a past...

The air and the wet and the cold take their toll.
Mushy and moldy, too squishy to roll.

The daylight gets shorter.
A sweater's in order!
A pumpkin falls into a pile.

A pumpkin is a miracle.
A hideaway miracle under the snow,
Sleeping and dreaming and ready to grow.

Thanks to one little friend,
Who was there 'til the end,
A pumpkin's an everyday miracle.

A pumpkin is a seed.
A plain little seed with a secret inside.
A pocket, a pip with a new life to hide.

And as the spring dawns
That one friend who held on –

Makes a pumpkin
That began
As a seed.

WELCOME TO THE PUMPKIN PATCH

PARTS OF A PUMPKIN

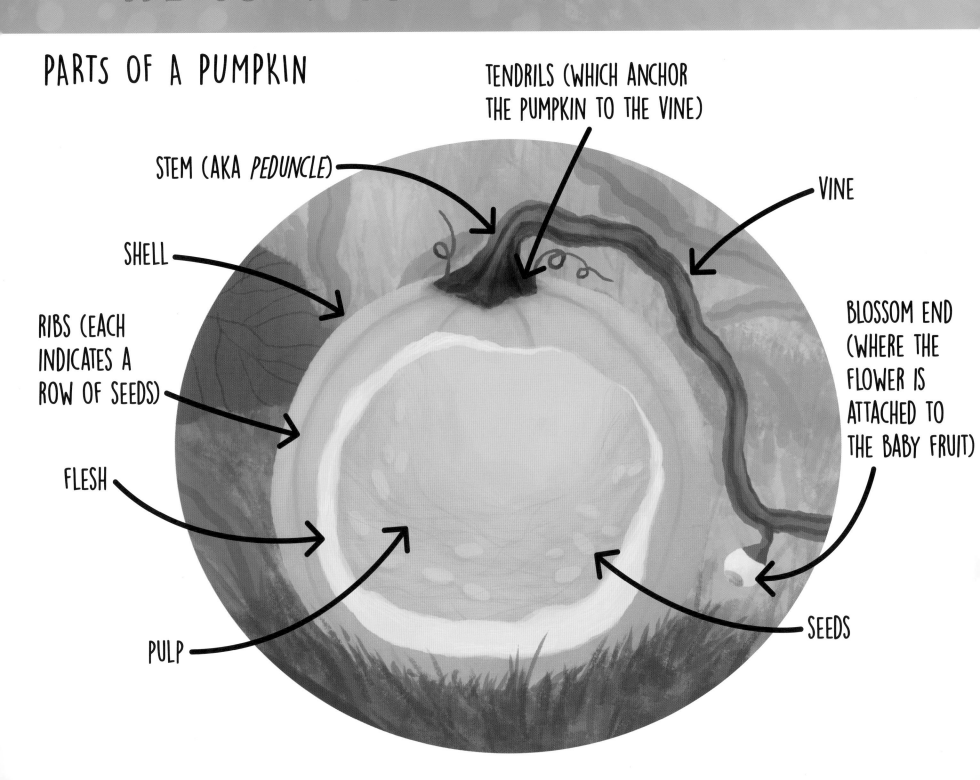

TENDRILS (WHICH ANCHOR THE PUMPKIN TO THE VINE)

STEM (AKA *PEDUNCLE*)

VINE

SHELL

RIBS (EACH INDICATES A ROW OF SEEDS)

BLOSSOM END (WHERE THE FLOWER IS ATTACHED TO THE BABY FRUIT)

FLESH

PULP

SEEDS

A PUMPKIN'S LIFE CYCLE

Did you know a pumpkin takes about one hundred days to grow? Pumpkins are *annuals,* which means they go through their entire life cycle in a single year. Every pumpkin follows the same steps.

Planting: Seeds get tucked into the soil after the last spring frost. The hard shell softens over time so the seed can sprout. Stay cozy, little seeds!

Germination: The main root, or *radicle*, pokes out of the seed coat and reaches downward. This root anchors the pumpkin in the soil and carries food and water to the seedling.

Sprouting: Two tiny leaves push their way out of the top of the seed coat and up, up, up through the soil. These leaves (called *cotyledons*) help the plant absorb warm spring sunlight so it can grow.

True Leaves: The pumpkin plant produces two larger leaves, and then a third, which take in even more sunlight to feed the plant. This process is called *photosynthesis.*

Roots: The system of small roots under the soil spreads out to deliver minerals and water they absorb from the ground.

Vine: The pumpkin plant concentrates on forming its vine, growing new leaves, and storing resources to use as it gets bigger. Once it really gets going, a pumpkin vine can grow six inches a day!

Flowering: About ten weeks after planting, yellow blossoms appear on the vines. These flowers open for a few hours every morning, hoping to attract bees and other insects to carry pollen from one flower to another.

Pollination: Pumpkin pollen is very sticky and heavy, so the best pollinators for pumpkins are bees. Lots of different kinds of bees work on pumpkins: honeybees, bumblebees, squash bees, carpenter bees, cuckoo bees, and sweat bees!

Fruit Set: If the bees do their job (thank you, bees!), a pumpkin will begin to grow. It will stay green for almost two months as it gets bigger and bigger.

Ripening: Once the pumpkin has grown big enough, a substance called *ethylene* tells the pumpkin to stop growing and start changing color. Most pumpkins turn orange, but some varieties turn red, blue, or white.

Senescence: The pumpkin is fully developed, and all its seeds are inside, so it doesn't need the vine or leaves anymore. Time to go pumpkin picking!

FUNGUS IN THE FIELD

Once a pumpkin is fully grown, it might get picked or left in the field. It might get chomped on by an animal or bruised on its way to the store. Whatever happens, even perfect pumpkins can't last forever! When a pumpkin starts to soften and rot, the process is called *decomposition*.

Decomposition will happen faster with the help of warm air and moisture. If you live somewhere that's still warm in late October, carve a pumpkin and leave it on your porch to watch the magic happen!

In decomposition, tiny organisms like mold and fungus will begin to grow in the pumpkin. They might look like little black dots or white fur. As the fungus decomposes the pumpkin, the pumpkin will change colors, shrink, sag, and eventually fall apart.

If you let your pumpkin rot in a garden or in a big pot with soil underneath it, you can cover it with more soil, and soon, you'll see little sprouts poking through. All the mushy goodness of your old pumpkin will feed your new plants...and you can grow a new pumpkin for next year!

FUNGUS IN THE FOREST

Fungus doesn't just help this year's pumpkins grow next year's pumpkins. It also plays an important role in places like forests by decomposing the wood in trees.

Sometimes when a tree dies, it might seem like a good idea to cut it down. But dead trees (also called *snags*) can be:

- A room for flying squirrels, bats, owls, woodpeckers, and other birds to spend the night in.

- A home where cavity-nesting birds like owls, woodpeckers, nuthatches, chickadees, wrens, sparrows, and flycatchers can raise a family.

- A perch for raptors like hawks and owls to sit and watch for trouble . . . or lunch!

- A treasure trove full of shredded wood for nest-building and yummy insects for eating.

- A storage bin for winter supplies like nuts for squirrels and chipmunks.

Decaying wood is the perfect place for fungi to feed new trees as they grow. It might seem sad to see a mushy pumpkin or a dead tree, but remember, without decomposition, a really important part of the life cycle would be missing!

A ROTTEN WALK IN THE WOODS

You can take a nature walk and look for signs of rot and decay in the woods! Here's what to watch for:

 Trees that have fallen down or split.

Fun fact! Decay in trees has different names depending on which part of the tree is rotting: *top rot* is at the top, *stem rot* or *trunk rot* is in the middle, and *root rot* or *butt rot* is at the bottom. (Go ahead. Try not to giggle!)

 Fungus on fallen trees or stumps.

Fun fact! There are thousands of kinds of fungus—some look like round puffballs, while others form layers of plates that look like clams. Some are white, some are black, others are pink or brown or yellow. They have fun names like "chicken of the woods," and some fungi are edible! (Note: Unless you are with an expert forager, you should never, ever eat anything you find in the woods because you could get very sick.)

 Insects crawling on or under rotten logs.

Fun fact! Certain insects and plants live in rotting wood and help break it down, putting nutrients back into the soil to help new forest plants to grow. Look closely at a rotten log and you might find centipedes, woodlice, longhorn beetles, ferns, mosses, and lichens.

PUMPKIN FUN FACTS AND FOOD!

DID YOU KNOW?

- Pumpkins grow on six out of seven continents. (Sorry, Antarctica!)

- Pumpkins are members of the *cucurbit* family. That means they're related to cucumbers, squashes, and watermelons.

- Every single part of a pumpkin is edible. Yep, you can eat the skin, leaves, flowers, pulp, seeds, and even the stem! (I'll stick with pie, thanks.)

- The tradition of carving jack-o-lanterns comes from Ireland. The Irish originally carved turnips and potatoes, but when they immigrated to America, they found it was much easier to use pumpkins.

- The world record for the heaviest pumpkin is held by a man in Italy. He grew one in 2021 that weighed 2,702 pounds!

- The largest pumpkin pie ever made was over five feet in diameter and weighed over three hundred and fifty pounds. It used eighty pounds of cooked pumpkin, thirty-six pounds of sugar, and twelve dozen eggs and took six hours to bake.

RECIPE FOR ROASTED PUMPKIN SEEDS

Pumpkins are grown and used in delicious dishes all over the world, from stews to custards to breads. One of the simplest ways to celebrate the diversity of the pumpkin is to roast its seeds and season them in your own way.

SEASONINGS FROM AROUND THE WORLD

Curry powder (India)   Oregano (Italy)

Cinnamon (Madagascar)   Cardamom (Egypt)

Paprika (Spain)   Chile powder (Mexico)

INGREDIENTS

- 2 cups fresh pumpkin seeds
- 3 tablespoons melted butter or coconut oil
- 2 teaspoons seasoning (Choose from the list or invent your own combination.)
- 1 teaspoon salt

YOU WILL NEED

- A sheet pan or cookie sheet
- Aluminum foil
- Three bowls: small, medium, and large
- A colander or strainer
- A cloth towel or paper towels
- A wooden spoon or spatula

MAKE YOUR SEEDS

- *Step 1:* Preheat the oven to 250°F. Line a sheet pan with aluminum foil, and lightly grease it with butter or oil.
- *Step 2:* Scoop all the seeds and pulp out of your pumpkin and put it all in a big bowl.
- *Step 3:* Separate the seeds from the pulp. Rinsing the seeds and pulp in a colander under cold running water will help loosen them.
- *Step 4:* Spread your clean seeds on a towel and dry them thoroughly. You can let them air-dry if you're patient or blot them with paper towels if you don't want to wait.
- *Step 5:* With a grown-up's help, melt your butter or coconut oil in a small pot on the stove. You can also melt it in the microwave on high for 30 seconds at a time.
- *Step 6:* Combine your seasonings with your melted butter or oil and a teaspoon of salt in a small bowl. Then drizzle the mixture over your dry pumpkin seeds in a medium bowl. Toss to combine.
- *Step 7:* Bake the seeds at 250°F for about 45 minutes, stirring occasionally.
- *Step 8:* Increase the oven temperature to 325°F, and bake for another 5 to 10 minutes. This will help make your seeds extra crunchy and delicious.
- *Step 9:* Let your seeds cool and then...start snacking!

HANNAH BARNABY is the author of multiple picture books and novels for children. She lives in Virginia, where she loves to hike with her dogs, and pumpkin season sometimes feels like summer. Her birthday is four days after Halloween, so she always has leftover candy—and roasted pumpkin seeds!—to enjoy with her birthday cake. You can visit her online at hannahbarnaby.com.

CÉDRIC ABT is a French illustrator whose work is a mix of traditional and digital techniques. For Cédric, the process is a sort of laboratory where experimentation and accidents give life to his drawings and create dreamlike and colorful universes. His creative journey is based on themes that generate inspiration: human nature, environmental nature, childhood, and more. He lives in Brittany in Northern France, closest to nature and the sea.